DOMINOES

From the Heart

LEVEL ONE   400 HEADWORDS

OXFORD
UNIVERSITY PRESS

Great Clarendon Street, Oxford OX2 6DP

Oxford University Press is a department of the University of Oxford.
It furthers the University's objective of excellence in research, scholarship,
and education by publishing worldwide in

Oxford New York

Auckland Cape Town Dar es Salaam Hong Kong Karachi
Kuala Lumpur Madrid Melbourne Mexico City Nairobi
New Delhi Shanghai Taipei Toronto

With offices in

Argentina Austria Brazil Chile Czech Republic France Greece
Guatemala Hungary Italy Japan Poland Portugal Singapore
South Korea Switzerland Thailand Turkey Ukraine Vietnam

OXFORD and OXFORD ENGLISH are registered trade marks of
Oxford University Press in the UK and in certain other countries

This edition © Oxford University Press 2010

The moral rights of the author have been asserted

Database right Oxford University Press (maker)

First published in Dominoes 2002

2014 2013 2012 2011 2010

10 9 8 7 6 5 4 3 2 1

ISBN: 978 0 19 424763 4 BOOK
ISBN: 978 0 19 424727 6 BOOK AND MULTIROM PACK
MULTIROM NOT AVAILABLE SEPARATELY

No unauthorized photocopying

Printed in China

ACKNOWLEDGEMENTS

Commissioned Photographs by: Gareth Boden

Illustrations by: Dominic Bugatto/Three in a Box

The publisher would like to thank the following for their time and assistance: Locations provided by
Freud Café, Walton Street, Oxford; Aquavitae Restaurant, 1 Folly Bridge, Oxford OX1 4LB;
Brookes University, Oxford (climbing wall). Models provided by Mad Dog Casting and Jackie
Palmer Agency

The publisher would like to thank the following for permission to reproduce photographs: Getty
Images pp6 (Oxford skyline/Travelpix Ltd), 7 (Dance floor/Simon Wilkinson), 38 (helicopter/
Matthew McVay), 38 (Matterhorn/Lythgoe); Mark Mason Studios p38 (climbing helmet);
OUP pp24 (Climber), 38 (Wedding ring/Photodisc), 38 (flowers), 39 (Worn boots/Photodisc).

With special thanks to all the team not mentioned above who helped to make this book.

DOMINOES

Series Editors: Bill Bowler and Sue Parminter

From the Heart

Alan C. McLean

Alan C. McLean has written stories for readers of all ages. He was born in Scotland, but has lived and worked in a number of countries, including Zambia, Venezuela and Nepal, where he trekked to Everest Base Camp. He works as an editor and teacher-trainer and has recently run workshops for writers in Uzbekistan and Uganda. He enjoys hill-walking and skiing, and likes cooking and playing the piano.

OXFORD
UNIVERSITY PRESS

BEFORE READING

1 **This is Anna. She is a student at Oxford University.
Who are these people? Match the names with the photos.**

a ☐ Sebastian, a rich student at Oxford University

b ☐ Derek, Anna's father

c ☐ Jane, Derek's friend

d ☐ Selim, a barman from Bosnia

2 **In Chapter 1, who says . . .?**

Two beers and a Coke, please.

Phone me when you get to the university.

c ....

a ....

d ....

You stupid girl!

I come from Sarajevo.

b ....

1 My first days at Oxford

The Oxford **bus** was late. I looked at Dad and he looked at me. I didn't speak. What could I say? It was good that Jane was there.

'Phone me when you get to the **university**, Anna,' Dad said.

'Of course, Dad.'

Jane smiled and took my Dad's arm. 'Derek, Anna's going to be OK. She's a big girl now.'

'I know,' said Dad. 'But there are lots of not very nice people out there. **Foreigners**, most of them.'

'Dad!'

bus a big car that lots of people use to go from one place to another

university people study here after they finish school

foreigner a person who is not from your country

The bus came after about ten minutes. We all said goodbye and I got on. I sat down and watched Jane and Dad standing there in the cold, smiling at me. I liked Jane. She and Dad were good friends. They met at work. Of course, that was after Mum left us . . . but I didn't want to think about that.

Five minutes later the bus left, and with it I left Jane and Dad and my old home behind me. It was hot on the bus and I took off my new coat. It was a **present** from Dad, for **climbing** in Wales. 'We can go climbing again when you're in Oxford,' he said. We wanted to go back to Wales next month.

I looked out of the bus window and thought about Oxford. 'I'm going to be a student at Oxford University,' I thought. 'But am I going to like it?'

My first days at Oxford were exciting. Everything was new. I had a new room to live in, I **bought** lots of books and I met lots of new people. There were two girls living with me, Penny and Magda. Penny was from Manchester and Magda was from Germany. We were soon good friends.

At the end of the first week, there was a **dance** for the new students. Penny, Magda and I went to it. The music was good and I danced with some of the boys there, but they were all very young! Most of the time Penny, Magda and I danced together.

'It's hot in here,' said Penny. 'Let's go and get a drink.'

'Yes,' said Magda. 'I'm thirsty.'

'OK,' I said. 'Leave it to me!'

There were lots of people at the **bar**, but I **pushed** to the front. The young man behind the bar was tall with dark hair. 'He's good-looking,' I thought. Just then he looked at

present something that you give to someone

climb to go up using your hands and feet

buy (past **bought**) to give someone money for something

dance an evening with music where people can meet and have a good time; to move your body and feet to music

bar a place where people buy drinks

push to move quickly and strongly with your hands

me. He had beautiful blue eyes! Then he smiled.

'What would you like?' he asked. He spoke nicely, but he wasn't English. He was a foreigner. Where was he from?

'Two **beers** and a Coke, please,' I said.

'Two beers and a Coke,' he said, and he gave me the drinks. 'That's three pounds forty,' he smiled at me.

I gave him the money and I began to take the drinks back to Penny and Magda.

'Can I help you with those?' someone asked. 'One small young girl with three big drinks to carry. It isn't right!'

I looked up and saw a young man with a red face next to me at the bar. He looked **drunk**. I don't like drunk men.

I was angry but I spoke quietly. 'I can carry my drinks without your help, thank you very much.'

beer a yellow or brown drink

drunk when someone drinks a lot and can't speak well or stand without help

'You don't understand,' the man said. 'A young man must always help a young woman. My father told me once, "Sebastian, my boy," he said—'

'OK, Sebastian,' I said. 'I'm not interested in your father or in you. Can I get past?'

I began to walk past him, but he put his hand out to stop me. I pushed his arm away. Coke went all over Sebastian's shirt.

'You **stupid** girl!' he cried. 'Look at my beautiful shirt!'

Sebastian was very angry. He stood in front of me. His right arm went up. Suddenly I was afraid. 'He's going to hit me,' I thought.

stupid not thinking well

'Stop that at once!' someone said quietly. It was the man behind the bar. 'Don't hit that young woman.'

'Are you talking to me?' asked Sebastian. His face was redder than before.

'Yes, I am,' the **barman** said. 'And I ask you to be nice to that young woman. Men do not hit women in my country.'

'Your country? And what is your country?'

'I come from Bosnia,' the barman said.

'Oh so you're an **immigrant**,' Sebastian said. 'Well, can I tell you something? We don't want lots of immigrants in our country thank you very much. I say, do the **police** know you're here? Or are you an **illegal** immigrant?'

The barman didn't say anything.

'Do you know something?' said Sebastian. 'I think I'm going to call the police—'

Just then a young woman came up to the bar. She took Sebastian's arm.

'There you are,' she said. 'Come on, Sebastian. Klaus and Maria are waiting for us. They're over there. I say, Sebastian, what did you do to your shirt?'

The young woman and Sebastian began to walk away.

'I tell you, Ginny. I'm going to call the police. That barman—'

'Don't be stupid, Sebby. Come along now.'

Ginny and Sebastian went back to their friends. I looked at the barman.

'Thanks for your help,' I said.

'That's all right,' he said.

'So was that true?' I asked. '*Are* you from Bosnia?'

'Yes, I am. I come from Sarajevo and my name is Selim.'

barman a man who works in a bar

immigrant someone who comes from their home country to live in a different country

police they look for people who break the law

illegal something that is against the law

5

ACTIVITIES

READING CHECK

Are these sentences true or false? Tick the boxes.

		True	False
a	Jane is Anna's mother.	☐	☑
b	Anna sometimes goes climbing with her father.	☐	☐
c	Penny and Magda are Anna's friends in Oxford.	☐	☐
d	Anna dances with Selim.	☐	☐
e	Sebastian helps Anna to carry her drinks.	☐	☐
f	Sebastian is angry with Anna.	☐	☐
g	Selim hits Sebastian.	☐	☐

WORD WORK

1 Complete the puzzle with words from Chapter 1.

```
p  o  l  i  c  e
         l     g     l
f     r     g  n     r  s
   b     r        n
         b     s
      u  n     v     r     t  y
p  r     s     t
   m  m     g  r     n
```

2 Use the letters in the blue squares to make one more word from Chapter 1. Anna and her father like doing this.

c _ _ _ _ _ _ _

3 Use the words from Activity 1 to complete the sentences.

a Anna is a student at Oxford <u>University</u>.

b Selim isn't from Britain. He's an .... from Bosnia.

c Sebastian thinks Selim can't work in Britain. He's going to tell the .... about him.

d Anna's coat is a .... from her father. He gave it to her before she left for Oxford.

e Anna's father doesn't like .... He only likes British people.

f Selim is working in Oxford. He's a .... there.

g It is .... to drive a car when you are drunk.

h It's usually cheaper to go by .... than to go by train.

4 **Use these words to complete the sentences.**

drunk stupid buy push dance beer bar

a I'm going to the shops to ......buy...... some bread.

b You can't talk and you can't stand up – and what's that bottle in your hand? I think you're ....

c Don't be .... Two and two aren't five!

d Oh, this is nice music. Would you like to .... with me?

e It's hot and I'm very thirsty. Let's have a ....

f Last summer I worked in a .... in Italy, selling drinks to foreigners.

g I'm carrying all these bags and I need some help to get out. Can you .... the door open for me?

GUESS WHAT

What do we learn about Selim in the next chapter? Tick four boxes.

a ☐ He is an illegal immigrant.

b ☐ It wasn't easy for him to stay in Bosnia.

c ☐ He learned English in Bosnia.

d ☐ He came to England to be with his friends.

e ☐ His mother and father live in Bosnia.

f ☐ He likes climbing.

2 Selim's story

Selim smiled at me again. Just then Penny and Magda came to the bar.

'Have you got the drinks?' Penny asked.

'Yes, sorry,' I said. 'Someone pushed me and I lost the Coke.'

'Here you are,' said Selim. And he gave me a new Coke. He quickly put a small **paper** into my hand, too. I put the paper in my bag and gave the Coke to Penny.

We sat and finished our drinks. Some time later Magda looked at her watch.

'I'd like to go now,' she said. 'I'm tired.'

So we went.

When I got home, I took the paper out of my bag and opened it. It had a telephone number on it and next to it, in big letters: *PHONE ME – SELIM.*

paper you write on this

Next day I phoned Selim. I wanted to see him again. I wanted to know more about him. I knew something about Bosnia, but I wanted to know more. Why was he in Britain? Was he an illegal immigrant or not?

I was interested in Selim's story. But there was something more. I remembered his blue eyes and his nice smile. When I thought of Selim, I felt excited!

We met one afternoon and walked along the river. It was a sunny day. We came to a **café** next to the river. We had some coffee and sat and talked. I asked him about Bosnia.

'Do your mother and father live in Sarajevo?'

Selim closed his eyes. 'My mother and father are dead,' he said. 'They died in the streets of Sarajevo. One day they went to the shops to buy things to eat. There was a **bomb** in the street and it killed them.'

'Oh, Selim, I'm sorry,' I said. What could I say?

café a place where people go to drink coffee

bomb a thing which explodes noisily and can kill people and break buildings

'I stayed in Bosnia to find work. But there was no work in Sarajevo. And it was **dangerous** for me there. People wanted to kill me. There was nothing for me in Bosnia. I knew English from school. So I came to Britain.' He laughed. 'I gave a friend a lot of money to bring me here. But now, here in Britain, they say, "Go back to Bosnia."'

'But it was dangerous for you to be in Bosnia. You said that.'

'Yes, I tell them this, but then they say, "You are in Britain because you want to work here, not because Bosnia was dangerous." So now I am an illegal immigrant and I am afraid of the police.'

'But how can you find work here?'

'It's not easy to find work. And the work is not good. When there was work in Bosnia I worked with computers. Here I work in bars and cafés. I say, "I am Greek." Greek people can work here, but not Bosnians. So here in Britain I am Greek.'

Selim laughed again. But it wasn't a happy laugh. We drank our coffee and looked at the river.

'Do you **miss** Bosnia?' I asked.

'Sometimes. I miss the **mountains**. In Bosnia every weekend I went to the mountains. I love climbing.'

'But that's wonderful!' I said. 'I love climbing, too. My Dad and I are climbers.'

'But there are no mountains here,' Selim said.

'Not in Oxford, no. But there are mountains in Wales. That's not very far away. My dad and I are going to climb in Wales next month.'

Then I thought of something.

'Selim, listen,' I said. 'There's a climbing **wall** in the

dangerous that can kill you

miss to want something that you once had, but that you don't have now

mountains very big hills

wall the side of a room

fun that you like doing

route the way to get from one place to another place

rope a very strong, thick string

university. It's good **fun**. Let's go and climb there next week.'

So next week we met at the university climbing wall. Selim looked up at it.

'This is new to me,' he said. 'We don't have climbing walls in Bosnia.'

'It's easy,' I said. 'Watch me.'

I climbed one of the easy **routes** up the wall. Selim watched me. Then he did it.

He was good. I could see that. He moved easily up the wall. When he came down, he smiled.

'I liked that,' he said. 'You're right. It was fun. But it was very easy. Let's try a different route.'

So we tried a different, longer route. This time we had **ropes**. I went first. Selim came after me. I'm a good climber, but Selim was better than me.

When we finished, Selim said, 'That was good. Can we do it again? Perhaps next week?'

I looked at him and smiled happily. 'I'd like that,' I said.

READING CHECK

1 Choose the right words to finish the sentences.

a Anna . . .

   1 ☐ phones her father.

   2 ☑ phones Selim.

   3 ☐ gets a phone call from Selim.

b Selim and Anna . . .

   1 ☐ meet in a café.

   2 ☐ walk along the river.

   3 ☐ meet in the university.

c Selim says that his parents died . . .

   1 ☐ in their house.

   2 ☐ in a Bosnian café.

   3 ☐ in a street in Sarajevo.

d Anna asks Selim . . .

   1 ☐ to go climbing with her.

   2 ☐ to go to the cinema with her.

   3 ☐ to study at the university with her.

2 What did Selim do in Bosnia? What does he do in Oxford? Tick the boxes.

a

☑ Bosnia
☐ Oxford

d

☐ Bosnia
☐ Oxford

b

☐ Bosnia
☐ Oxford

e

☐ Bosnia
☐ Oxford

c

☐ Bosnia
☐ Oxford

f

☐ Bosnia
☐ Oxford

ACTIVITIES

WORD WORK

1 Match the words with the pictures.

a wall

b paper

c mountains

d rope

e café

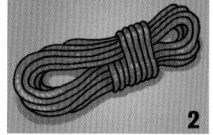

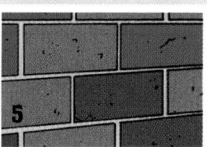

2 Use the words from the climbing wall to complete the sentences.

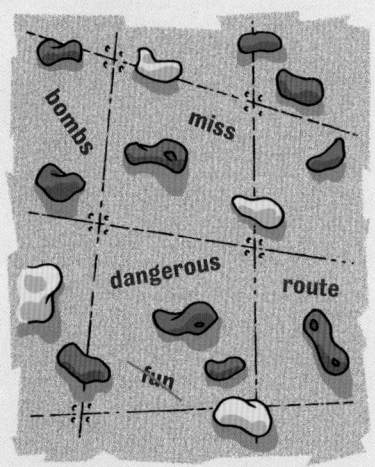

a I like watching TV in Britain. It's a lot of
...fun... .

b I really .... my country. I often think of
my home and want to be there.

c Let's try the easy .... up this climbing
wall. Climb up on the left and then climb across
to the right.

d Life in Sarajevo was .... for Selim.
There were .... in the street and many
people died.

GUESS WHAT

In the next chapter, Anna speaks to her Dad on the phone. What does she say about Selim?

a ☐ 'I met a nice boy. He likes climbing.'

b ☐ 'I met a very nice boy. He's called Selim and he's from Bosnia.'

c ☐ Nothing.

3 About my father

My Dad phoned that evening.

'How are you?' he asked. 'How is it going?'

'Good, Dad,' I said. 'I'm having a wonderful time here.

'Don't forget our visit to Wales.'

'No, Dad. Of course not. You know, I went to the university climbing wall today and it was good fun. We had a nice time.'

'Did you go with one of your friends?'

'Well . . . yes, I did. Look, Dad, I must go now. Penny's here and she's waiting for me to finish. We're going to make dinner tonight. We can speak again next week. Goodbye, now.'

Of course, Penny wasn't there. But I couldn't tell Dad about Selim. Why not? Well, for you to understand, I think I need to tell you something about my father.

His name is Derek, Derek Palmer. He works in a **factory**. It's a Swedish factory and it makes **mobile** phones, Lundberg phones. Perhaps you know the name. It's a big factory and lots of people work there. Dad is a **manager** in the factory. In fact, he's the **sales** manager. He's a good worker, but last year sales weren't very good. He told me about it one day.

'You see,' he said, 'in Britain more than 70% of the people have mobile phones. So now we're selling to

factory a building where lots of people make things

mobile that you can take with you

manager a person who organizes the work of other people

sales the number of things that you sell

14

only 30% of the people. What are we going to do when everyone has a mobile phone?'

So Dad was **worried** about his work. But that wasn't the only thing.

Lundberg is a big **company**. It has some British managers and some Swedish managers. One of the Swedish managers was called Lars. He and Dad became friends, good friends. They often went out for drinks together. Then Lars began to come round to our house for dinner. Mum, Dad, and Lars did lots of things together. Mum – Jill is her name – wasn't interested in climbing. She liked going to the cinema. Lars liked that too. So Mum and Lars began to go to the cinema together. They usually went to the cinema at weekends. Most weekends Dad and I went climbing.

I can never forget one weekend – that weekend when everything went wrong. Dad and I came back on Sunday

worried not happy about something and thinking a lot about it

company a group of people all working to make or do something for money

night as usual. It was late, and the house was dark. Mum wasn't there. I looked downstairs. Dad went upstairs to look for her. I felt worried. Where was she? 'Perhaps she went for a drink with Lars,' I thought.

Then I heard a cry from upstairs. I went up and opened the door of Mum and Dad's room. Dad was there on the bed with his back to me. I went to him. When he looked up at me, his eyes were red. He had a letter in his hand.

'What's wrong, Dad? What is it?'

He said nothing but gave me the letter. I didn't want to read it.

'She left with Lars,' Dad said. '"I love him," she says. Did you know anything about this, Anna?'

'No, Dad. Of course not.'

'What am I going to do without her?'

I felt afraid. I walked over to Dad and **hugged** him. We cried a lot that night.

Mum didn't come back. Lars got a job in Sweden and Mum went with him. Dad was very quiet about it all at first. Then he began to get angry. He was angry with Mum, but he was angrier with Lars. Lars was his friend, he thought. How could a friend do that to you? Then he found an answer to that question. It was because Lars was a foreigner, he said. British people didn't do that to their friends. Only foreigners did that.

Of course, that isn't true. British people aren't different from people from other countries. I told Dad that again and again. But I couldn't make him think differently. After Mum left, he **hated** foreigners. And he hated immigrants most of all.

'They come here and they take our **jobs**,' he said. 'Then they take our women, too. I'd like them all to go back home.'

Maybe Dad's going to change now he's got Jane. She came to work at Lundberg a month after Mum left us. I think Jane's good for Dad. She's very different from Mum, but that's OK with me. I can talk to Jane, but I can't talk to Dad and I didn't want to tell him about Selim.

hug to take in your arms lovingly

hate not to like

job work

ACTIVITIES

READING CHECK

Correct the mistakes in these sentences.

a Derek works for a ~~Japanese~~ *Swedish* company.

b Lundberg makes computers.

c All the people in Britain have mobile phones.

d Lars comes from Wales.

e Lars and Derek weren't good friends at first.

f Anna's Mum liked climbing.

g Lars and Jill went out for drinks together.

h Lars left a letter for Derek.

i Anna hugged her Mum on the night Jill left with Lars.

j Anna can talk easily to her Dad about Selim.

WORD WORK

Use the letters to make words. Then write the sentences.

a Derek Palmer works for a **anompyc** called Lundberg.

... Derek Palmer works for a company called Lundberg. ..

b He has a good **bjo** with Lundberg.

. . . .

c He's a **leass regnaam** .

. . . .

d Lundberg make and **lesl lebmoi** phones.

. . . .

18

e They have **trcfaosei** in England and in Sweden.

. . . .

f Derek is **redowri** about his work.

. . . .

g After Jill left him, Derek began to **thea** foreigners.

. . . .

GUESS WHAT

What happens in the next chapter? Tick the boxes.

a Selim gets a letter. What does it say?

1 ☐ He has a new job.

2 ☐ He can stay in Britain.

3 ☐ He must leave Britain.

b Anna and Derek go climbing together. What happens?

1 ☐ Selim goes with them.

2 ☐ Anna tells Derek about Selim.

3 ☐ Anna wants to tell Derek about Selim, but she can't.

4 My climbing weekend

I saw a lot of Selim in the next month or two. I liked him a lot. He was good-looking. But he had more than good looks. Selim was **kind**. His English wasn't always right but he was easy to be with and easy to talk to. But one day when we met he was angry. He had a letter with him.

'Look at this,' he said. 'I must go. I must leave England. Now I must go back to Bosnia.'

'But why? What happened?'

'Someone told them about me. They saw me working in a café. "He is not Greek," they said. "He is an illegal immigrant."'

He turned to me.

kind nice to people

'Why do they hate me?' he asked. 'I don't understand. I don't want to take money from this country. I don't want something for nothing. I only want to live here and work. I am a man. I feel things. I have a **heart**. Why are British people afraid of me?'

'I don't know,' I said. 'Some British people don't like foreigners. You're different from them. And they don't like different people. Don't think about them, Selim. Think about me. I like you.'

I **kissed** him, but he didn't kiss me back. He was very angry.

Some days later Selim was angry again when I told him about my climbing weekend with Dad.

'Please stay with me this weekend,' he said.

'I'm sorry, Selim, but my father and I **planned** this visit to Wales a long time ago.'

'You are **lucky** to have a father,' Selim said. Now he was **sad**. 'My father is dead. He died with my mother five years ago this week. It was on October 26. This Saturday.'

'Oh, Selim, I'm sorry. I didn't know that. I'd like to be with you then. But I must go with my father. Can't you understand that?'

'So you're going to leave me here,' Selim said.

I didn't say a thing. And Selim sat and watched me, sad and angry, and said nothing. In the end we said goodbye and I didn't see him again that week.

Dad came to get me from university on Friday afternoon and we drove to Wales. He was happy and excited. Dad was always happy when he went climbing. In the car we talked about our weekend.

heart the centre of feeling in somebody

kiss to touch with your mouth lovingly

plan to want to do something; to get something ready before doing it

lucky when something happens that is good for you

sad not happy

'I want to climb Tryfan,' he said.

I didn't speak. Tryfan isn't a very big mountain, but it isn't easy to climb.'

Dad looked at me.

'We can do it, Anna,' he said.

'I don't know. Let's see, Dad,' I answered.

Early next morning it was warm and the sun was hot. But soon the sun went in and the sky got darker and darker. As we walked across country up to Tryfan, it began to rain. There are some dangerous **rocks** on Tryfan and now they were **wet**. Dad went first. His feet **slipped** on the wet rock and he stopped. Now I went up past him. I could see the route up the mountain, but it wasn't going to be easy. Then I looked back down. Dad had the rope in his hands, but he was tired. Could he climb up? I didn't think he could. I called down to him.

'I can't do it, Dad. I'm going to come down.'

Dad and I sat there under the rocks. We ate our sandwiches and drank our coffee. The rain was worse than before.

'Let's climb Tryfan another day, Dad,' I said.

'OK. We can come back here again. Perhaps at **Easter** when the weather's better. What do you think?'

'Yes. Let's come back at Easter,' I said.

We talked some more. Dad was happy. Happier than usual, I thought. Perhaps it was a good time to tell him about Selim.

'Dad . . .?' I began.

'Yes, Anna.'

'There's a boy at the university . . .' No, that wasn't right. I began again.

rock a very big stone

wet with water on it

slip to move very quickly on something wet

Easter a spring holiday

'Dad, I've got a friend at the university,' I said. 'A boy . . .'

'A boyfriend! Well, I must say, that was quick,' Dad said and he smiled. 'Tell me about him.'

'Well, he's got dark hair and blue eyes . . .'

Dad laughed. 'Yes, yes, that's all very interesting, but tell me, is he a nice boy?'

'Yes, dad, he's nice, and kind. Oh, and he's a climber, too. He's a good climber. We went to the university climbing wall last week.'

'That's good, that's good. Well, maybe we can climb together. What's his name?'

'. . . Sam,' I said. 'His name's Sam.'

Well, what could I say? Selim isn't an English name, after all. And you know about my dad and foreigners!

READING CHECK

1 Tick the correct answers.

a Why does Anna like Selim?
  1 ☐ He's rich.
  2 ☑ He's good-looking and kind.
  3 ☐ He's an immigrant.

b What does Selim's letter say?
  1 ☐ He must go back to Bosnia.
  2 ☐ He can stay in Britain.
  3 ☐ He must get a different job.

c Why is the weekend important for Selim?
  1 ☐ He wants to climb with Anna.
  2 ☐ His mother and father died five years ago on that day.
  3 ☐ He wants to meet Anna's father.

d Why doesn't Anna stay with Selim at the weekend?
  1 ☐ She doesn't love him.
  2 ☐ She is angry with him.
  3 ☐ She's going climbing with her father.

2 Are these sentences true or false? Tick the boxes.

	True	False
a Derek wants to climb Tryfan.	☑	☐
b Tryfan is a big mountain.	☐	☐
c It's good weather for climbing.	☐	☐
d Derek slips on the rocks.	☐	☐
e Anna can see a route up the mountain.	☐	☐
f Anna tells Derek to climb up to her.	☐	☐
g They are going to come back to Tryfan at Easter.	☐	☐
h Anna tells Derek everything about Selim.	☐	☐

WORD WORK

Find words in the rope and complete the sentences.

a I like Selim because he's ......*kind*...... ; he has a good ....
and he's always nice to people when they need help.

b 'I hate going to work every day. You're .... to be a student!'

c With tears in her eyes she .... him goodbye and left.

d Dad .... this visit to Tryfan and phoned the hotel weeks ago.

e 'Be careful Dad! The mountain is very .... after all the rain!'

f My friend Dave .... on a wet .... and broke his leg.

g She's .... because she doesn't have many friends.

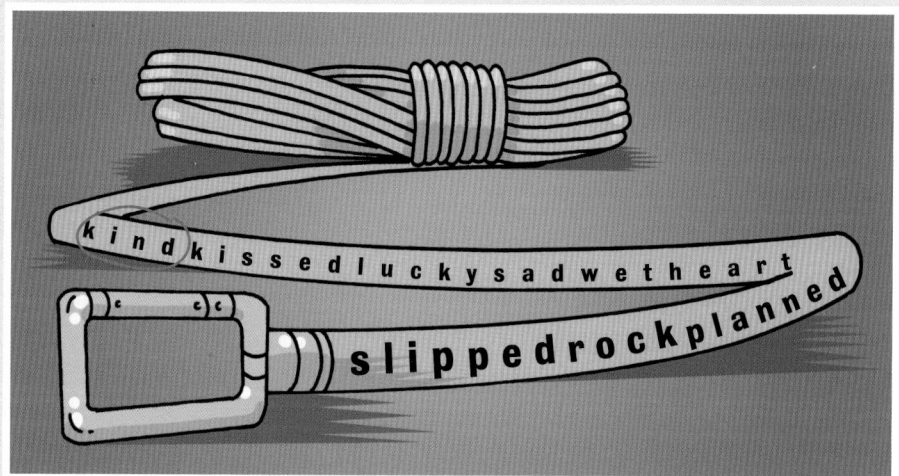

GUESS WHAT

What happens in the next chapter? Tick the boxes.

	Yes	No
a Anna stays in Oxford for Christmas.	☐	☐
b Derek is worried about the Lundberg factory closing down.	☐	☐
c Selim leaves Britain.	☐	☐
d Anna and Derek talk angrily about Selim.	☐	☐
e Selim tells Anna he doesn't want to see her again.	☐	☐

5 Home for Christmas

In the next weeks I forgot about Selim, about Dad, and about climbing. I stayed in my room and I worked hard. I had **exams** in December, and I was worried about them. I wanted to do well.

Then one day Selim came to see me. He was very worried.

'They sent me a new letter,' he said. 'Now I must leave Britain in two months. I can't go back to Bosnia. What can I do?'

'Selim,' I said, 'there's an **organization** in Oxford called Immigrant **Aid**. They help people like you. Magda told me about it. She gave me their phone number. Would you like it?'

'Can they help me?'

'Yes, of course they can, Selim. We don't all hate immigrants in Britain.'

'Don't you?'

'Look, Selim, I don't want to **argue** with you,' I said. 'Here's the phone number. Give them a call.'

My exams were not easy, but I answered most of the questions, so I was happy. But I was very tired. I went home for Christmas.

Dad wasn't there to meet me at the bus station, but Jane met me. We hugged.

'Why isn't Dad here? Is something wrong?'

'It's the factory, Anna. They're going to close it. Lundberg are going to make all their phones in Sweden now. Your father is very angry. "It's those foreigners again," he says.'

'He always says that. It's **rubbish**!'

'Don't be angry with your father, Anna. Try to be nice to him. He loves you. Things aren't easy for him now.'

'I know that, Jane. But . . .' And then I began to cry and I couldn't stop.

'What's the matter, Anna? You can tell me.'

And I told her about Selim. It was easy to tell Jane.

'It's OK, Anna,' she said. 'I understand. But I don't know about your father. Don't say anything to him at the moment,' she went on. 'It's not a good time. He's very worried about his job.'

'Can't we do something about the factory?' I asked. 'Can't we stop it closing? Can't we make Lundberg change their plans.'

'I said that to your dad, but he didn't listen. "There's nothing we can do," he told me. But I think we can do something about it. And I'm going to try,' said Jane.

Well, I tried to be nice to Dad. The first day or two he was fine. But on Christmas Day we argued. He began to talk about the factory again.

rubbish stupid things that are not true

'It's these immigrants,' he said. 'They come here and they take our jobs. And then British people can't find work.'

'Dad, that's rubbish. We need immigrants to work here. They work hard. They do the dirty jobs. You know, I like immigrants. I think they bring colour and new **life** to this country.'

'Oh, you like immigrants, do you? Perhaps you've got some immigrant friends in Oxford?'

'Derek . . .' said Jane.

'Yes, I have!' I went on, angrily. 'I told you about my boyfriend. Do you remember, Dad? Well, his name isn't Sam – it's Selim, and he's from Bosnia. Yes, Dad, my boyfriend's an immigrant. And I love him. How do you like that?'

life something moving and exciting

Dad's face went white. He left the room quickly. Jane followed him.

That evening I had a call from Selim. 'Happy Christmas, Anna,' he said to me.

'Oh, Selim, I'm having a terrible Christmas,' I said. 'My Dad and I argued.'

'What did you argue about?' he asked.

'Oh, nothing important,' I said. 'But what about you? Did you have a good Christmas?'

'Very good, Anna,' he said. 'I'm very happy. They're going to let me stay here for three more months. Immigrant Aid are going to help me. They told me about it on Monday. I tried to phone and tell you before.'

'Selim, that's wonderful. I'm very happy for you.'

'Anna, I love you.'

'I love you too, Selim. And I want to be with you now.'

I left home two days later and went back to Oxford.

I soon found a room in a house for Selim and me to **rent**. We were lucky. Some friends of Magda's left Oxford at New

rent to give money every month for somewhere to live

Year and we moved into their room. We were very happy there. Every day I went off to the university and he went off to his job at the café. We didn't have much money, but that was OK. We were in love.

I phoned home to tell Dad about it. But he was never there when I phoned. Perhaps he didn't want to speak to me. But I told Jane about Selim and me, and she was happy for us.

READING CHECK

1 Are these sentences true or false? Tick the boxes.   True   False

a Anna is worried about her exams.   ☑ ☐
b Derek meets Anna at the bus station.   ☐ ☐
c The Lundberg factory is going to close.   ☐ ☐
d Anna says that she hates immigrants.   ☐ ☐
e Selim can stay in Britain for six more months.   ☐ ☐
f Selim and Anna find a room in Oxford to live in.   ☐ ☐

2 Put these sentences in the correct order. Number them 1–8.

a ☐ Anna tells Jane about Selim.
b ☐ Selim phones Anna.
c ☐ Anna tells Derek about Selim.
d ☐ Anna goes home for Christmas.
e ☐ Anna tells Selim about Immigrant Aid.
f ☐ Anna and Derek argue.
g ☐ Selim starts to live with Anna.
h ☐ Anna goes back to Oxford to be with Selim.

WORD WORK

Use the words in the bus on page 31 to complete the sentences.

a At the end of the year I had ....exams.... . I studied a lot for them and I did well.
b When you are talking with someone and they say something stupid, it's easy to get angry and begin to .... with them.
c Countries with not much money sometimes get .... from richer countries to help them.
d Lots of people from different countries live in New York. They bring .... and colour to the city.
e You don't have the money to buy a house, so why don't you .... a room?
f My grandmother thinks that computers are dangerous, but that's ....
g UNICEF is a very good .... It helps children in different countries.

RENT

LIFE RUBBISH ~~EXAMS~~ aid

organization ARGUE

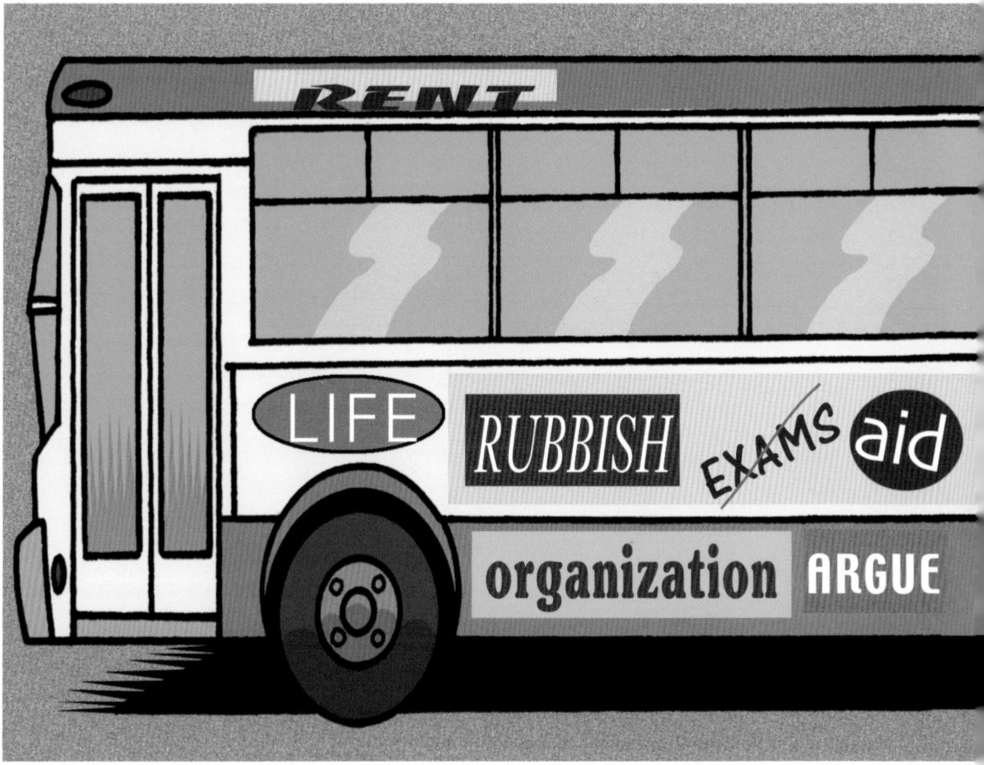

GUESS WHAT

What happens in the next chapter? Tick the boxes.

a Where does Derek meet Selim?
1 ☐ In a café.
2 ☐ In Derek's house.
3 ☐ In Anna and Selim's room.

b What do you think happens when Derek and Selim meet?
1 ☐ They argue.
2 ☐ Derek says he's sorry.
3 ☐ They talk happily for hours.

6 In love

I didn't hear from Dad for weeks. Then one Friday Jane phoned, and she and I talked. The next morning Dad and Jane came to see us in Oxford. Selim opened the door to them.

Dad wasn't very happy to see Selim, but Jane smiled at him and kissed me.

I asked them in, and we all sat down. I made some coffee and then we talked. Jane spoke first.

'We have something wonderful to tell you. It's about the Lundberg factory. It's not going to close now after all.'

'Thanks to you, love,' my father said. 'Tell them about it, Jane.'

'Well,' said Jane. 'I have a friend in the head office of Hayashi, the Japanese phone company. She told me that Hayashi want to open a new factory in Europe, so I told her about the Lundberg factory. They're buying the factory next month – and all the workers can stay.'

'That's wonderful!' I said. 'Isn't it, Selim?'

'There's something more,' Jane said. 'Derek wants to say something to Selim. Go on, Derek.'

'Yes,' said Dad. He spoke very quickly. 'Look, Selim. I said some stupid things about foreigners and immigrants. I'm sorry. But now I want us to be friends.'

'Yes,' said Selim. 'You love Anna and I love her, too. It's good for us to be friends.'

Selim got up and hugged Dad. At first, Dad's face went red, but then he smiled and hugged Selim back.

'Don't kiss him, Selim,' I said. Jane laughed.

'Right,' said Dad. 'Selim, I'd like you to come with

Anna and me to Wales at Easter.'

'And me,' said Jane. 'I'm coming too, remember.'

'Sorry. I forgot,' said Dad. 'That's right. We're all going to Wales.'

'Are we going to climb Tryfan?' Selim asked.

'Yes, we are!' I said before my father could speak.

'Good,' said Dad. And he smiled at Selim.

The weather at Easter was good. The sun was in the sky, but it wasn't very hot. There was some **wind**, but not very much. Jane drove us along the road to the foot of the mountains and we got out. We looked up at the mountains. Tryfan was beautiful in the sun. We were all excited.

'Look!' said Selim. 'I think Tryfan is a big animal. Now it is dead or sleeping. But perhaps one day it's going to come alive again.'

'It's a good day for climbing,' Dad said.

wind fast moving air

We said goodbye to Jane. She was going shopping in the next town.

'See you about five o'clock,' she said. 'Don't be late. Have a wonderful day. And be careful, Derek.'

We began to walk up to Tryfan. I could see the rock wall over our heads. I knew it was dangerous, but today the rock wasn't wet.

'It's going to be OK,' I thought.

And everything went well at first. We got the ropes out of our bags. Selim and I put **helmets** on. But Dad didn't.

'I don't need a helmet,' he said. 'I'll be OK without one.'

The sun went in. The wind was stronger now. Dad went first, then me, then Selim. Slowly we climbed up the big wall of rock. Dad was near the **top**.

'We're nearly there!' he called down to us.

Just then there was a big **gust** of wind. I looked up and suddenly a rock **fell** down from the top of the mountain.

'Dad!' I called.

But Dad didn't hear me. The rock hit him on the head. He fell. The rope went **tight** and I began to fall, too. There was nothing under me. I fell down, down, and then the rope went tight again and I stopped. I heard Selim's voice from far away.

helmet you wear this hard hat to stop your head from getting hurt

top the highest part of something

gust a sudden wind

fall (past **fell**) to go down quickly

tight straight and hard (of a rope)

'You're OK, Anna,' he called to me. 'I've got the rope. There's a big rock in front of you. Can you see it? **Swing** on the rope and **catch** it.'

I swung at the rock wall. Once, and once again. The third time I caught the big rock with my right hand.

'Good. Now climb down the wall of rock. It's easy. You can do it.'

I climbed slowly down the rock wall. I could see Dad now. His eyes were closed and he didn't move. Was he alive or dead?

Selim climbed down to me.

'It's all right,' he said. 'I can get to your father.'

Selim climbed down the rock to Dad. He looked at him carefully for a minute or two. Then he looked up, smiled, and called up to me.

'He's alive!'

I cried, but I was very happy.

Selim brought Dad back up to me. I found Dad's mobile phone and called the Mountain **Rescue** people. Then Selim put Dad on his back and we began to go down the

swing (past **swung**) to move from left to right on the end of a rope

catch (past **caught**) to take quickly in your hands

rescue taking someone away from something dangerous

mountain. I thought it all went on for hours, but it was only half an hour. I was tired and my arm felt bad. We moved very slowly. In the end we heard a **helicopter** above us. The Mountain Rescue people!

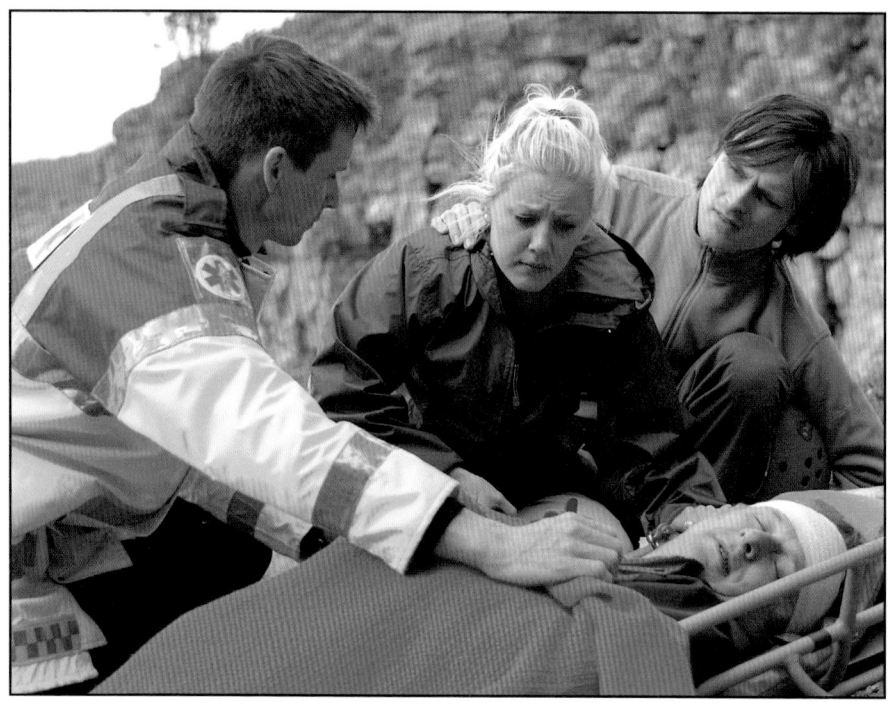

Just then we heard a cry. It was Jane. She ran towards us. 'Is it Derek?' she cried. 'Is he all right?'

'He's going to be OK now,' the Mountain Rescue man said. 'We're taking him to hospital.'

'Go with him, Jane,' I said. 'He needs you.'

Jane didn't say anything, but she hugged me. Then the Mountain Rescue people took her into the helicopter with Dad. They went off to the hospital.

Selim and I watched the helicopter. Then Selim spoke.

'Jane and your father – they are in love, yes?'

helicopter
something that flies with blades on top that go round and round

'Yes, they are in love,' I said. 'I'm happy for them.'

'What about us?' I thought. 'Are we in love, too?' I didn't know about us.

'I've got something for you,' Selim said. 'I'd like to give it to you now. It's a good time, I think.'

He brought out a small green box and gave it to me.

'Open it,' he said.

In the box there was a beautiful **ring**.

'It's from Bosnia,' Selim said. 'It was my mother's ring. My father gave it to her many years ago, before they were **married**. Now they are dead. Today I give it to you with love, Anna. It comes from me, from the heart.'

I took the ring and put it on the third finger of my left hand.

'Oh, Selim, it's beautiful,' I said. 'Thank you.'

I kissed him and took his hand.

'Let's go back down now,' I said.

ring a circle of metal that you wear on a finger

married having a husband or wife

READING CHECK

Correct nine more mistakes in the summary of this chapter.

Oxford

Jane and Derek come to see Anna and Selim in ~~London~~. Derek asks Selim to come climbing

with him and Anna. They go to climb Tryfan at Christmas. They get the ropes out and Derek

and Anna put on their climbing helmets. The sun goes in and the rain is stronger. Selim

goes up the mountain first. A rock falls down and hits Derek on the foot. Anna falls too, but

Selim holds the rope tight and she's OK. Selim climbs down to Derek. Derek is dead. Selim

calls the Mountain Rescue people on Anna's mobile phone. The Mountain Rescue helicopter

takes Derek and Jane to a hotel.

WORD WORK

1 These words don't match the pictures. Correct them.

a ~~top~~ helicopter ....

b rings ....

c helicopter ....

d wind ....

e helmet ....

2 Find words from Chapter 6 to complete the sentences making necessary changes.

a Suddenly a strong g u s t of wind hit me from behind.

b Tarzan s _ _ _ _ _ from tree to tree very easily.

c 'Does she have a husband?' 'No. She isn't m _ _ _ _ _ _.'

d He slipped on a rock and f _ _ _ down the mountain.

e I'd like to work in a mountain r _ _ _ _ _ organization, helping people when they have accidents on the mountains.

f The wind carried my hat down the road but I ran after it and c _ _ _ _ _ it.

g When Derek fell from the mountain, the rope between him and Anna suddenly went t _ _ _ _.

GUESS WHAT

What happens after the story ends?
Choose from these ideas or add your own.

a ☐ Anna and Selim get married.

b ☐ Jane and Derek get married.

c ☐ Selim goes back to Bosnia.

d ☐ Selim gets a good job in Britain.

e ☐ Anna leaves university.

f ☐ ....
....

g ☐ ....
....

h ☐ ....
....

PROJECT A

AN IMMIGRANT'S STORY

1 Read this letter from Maria, an immigrant worker in the USA, to her boyfriend Brad. Match the paragraphs and the pictures on page 41.

Dear Brad,

1 I'm sorry we argued last night. Please read this letter. Then you can understand me better.

2 Life in Mexico was terrible. When an earthquake killed my father and mother, I came to the USA. I gave a friend money to help me and she got papers for me to come here.

3 Life in Texas is different from life in Mexico City. I'm learning English and it isn't easy. Watching TV helps me a lot. And I have an American boyfriend – you – to help me. That's the best thing of all!

4 I'm a waitress here. I work in the evenings and at weekends. I'm sorry about getting angry when you talked to Carla. In Mexico it isn't usual for a man to talk to a woman in front of his girlfriend.

5 I get more money here than I got in Mexico for working in a hospital. But life is expensive here. I'm sorry I can't pay for more things, and I don't like taking your money, Brad. But thank you for helping me!

6 I like taking photos in my free time, and I think I'm lucky to know you, Brad, and your mother, Sandra, too. Thank you for taking me with you to see that photo exhibition.

Please let's meet and talk.

Your friend,

Maria

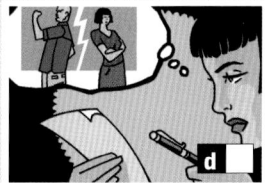

2 Now write a letter from Selim to Anna. Use Maria's letter and the words in the box to help you.

Bosnia   bomb

Oxford   Sarajevo

reading books

barman   Sebastian

computer company

climbing mountains

Tryfan   Derek

Dear Anna,

PROJECT B

Going walking

1 Anna went walking with her father last weekend. Look at the map and read her diary on page 43. Which route did they take?

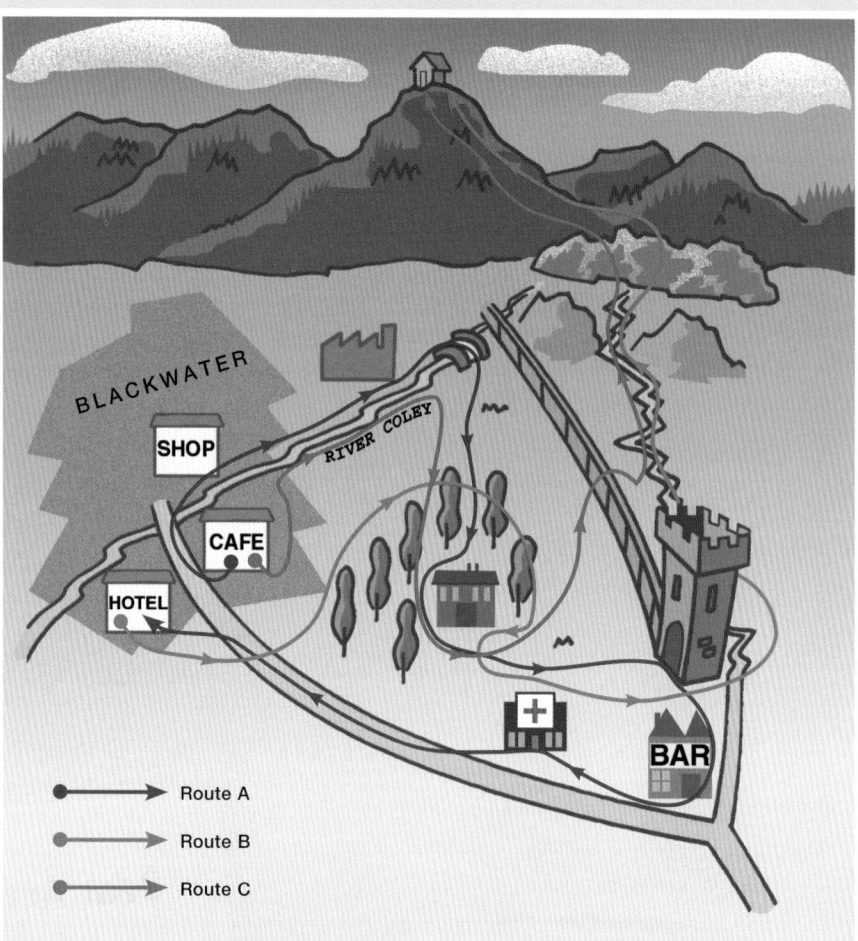

BLACKWATER

SHOP

CAFE

HOTEL

RIVER COLEY

BAR

Route A
Route B
Route C

We started at Blackwater village. We had breakfast in Blackwater Café. Then we walked out of the village along the River Coley. Soon we came to seven big old trees on the right. We walked between them to an old house. That's Seven Trees House. No one lives there now. After that we walked up to a wall. We climbed over the wall and turned left. Next we walked up an old road between two hills called High Door. We stopped and had a rest. Then we climbed up over some big rocks. That wasn't easy. In the end we climbed to the top of Blackwater Mountain. There's a little house up there. It was beautiful!

2 **Look at the map and choose a different route. Write about your walk like Anna. Use these phrases to help you.**

We started . . .

We had breakfast . . .

Then we walked . . .

Soon we came to . . .

We walked . . .

After that . . .

Next . . .

We stopped . . .

In the end . . .

3 Draw a map of a walk you remember well. (It can be in the country or in the town, your walk to school or a walk at the weekend.) Write about your walk. Use the diary and the phrases on page 43 to help you.

GRAMMAR

GRAMMAR CHECK

Prepositions

Prepositions of movement tell us how something moves.

along ▰▰▰➔   away ◣◢   into ➔▭   off ⌐●

on ⌐●   out of ▭➔   past ▭

Some verbs + prepositions have a special meaning.

come from (= originate from)   *get to* (= arrive)   *take off* (a coat)

Come, get, and take do not always take a preposition!

He came late.   *I got a letter.*   *She took some medicine.*

1 Complete the sentences with the prepositions in the box. Use some prepositions more than once.

along	at	away	from	into
off	on	out of	past	to

a Anna is going to phone her dad when she gets ....to.... university.

b Anna said goodbye to her dad and Jane and then she got .... the bus.

c On the bus, Anna took .... her coat and looked .... the window.

d Anna pushed .... people to get .... the bar.

e The barman looked .... Anna and she saw his beautiful blue eyes.

f Anna wanted to walk .... Sebastian but he stopped her.

g When Anna pushed Sebastian .... Coke went over his shirt.

h Sebastian and his friend walked .... from the bar.

i The barman told Anna that his name was Selim and he came .... Bosnia.

j Selim gave Anna a new Coke and put a small paper .... her hand.

k When Anna and Selim met, they walked .... the river.

GRAMMAR

GRAMMAR CHECK

Present Simple: Yes/No questions and short answers

We can answer Yes/No questions with a short answer.

We make an affirmative short answer by using subject pronoun + verb/auxiliary verb.

Is Anna a student?	*Yes, she is.*
Did Selim give Anna his phone number?	*Yes, he did.*
Can Selim climb well?	*Yes, he can.*

We make a negative short answer by using subject pronoun + verb/auxiliary verb + not. We usually use contractions in negative short answers.

Is Selim Greek?	*No, he isn't.*
Does Anna like Sebastian?	*No, she doesn't.*

2 **Write short answers for the questions about Chapter 2.**

   a Did Anna phone Selim? .... *Yes, she did.* ....

   b Was Anna interested in Selim's story? ....

   c Did Anna and Selim have coffee at a bar? ....

   d Are Selim's mother and father alive? ....

   e Was it dangerous to live in Sarajevo? ....

   f Is Selim an illegal immigrant? ....

   g Can Selim find work easily in Britain?

     ....

   h Did Selim work in a bar in Bosnia?

     ....

   i Does Selim miss the mountains in Bosnia?

     ....

   j Is Anna going climbing in Wales with Selim?

     ....

   k Is Selim good at climbing? ....

   l Is Anna better at climbing than Selim? ....

   m Is it the first time for Selim to climb on a climbing wall? ....

   n Does Selim want to meet Anna again? ....

GRAMMAR CHECK

Negative statements

We make the negative by adding not after the auxiliary verb do/does, and did in the Present or Past Simple tenses. Don't/doesn't and didn't are followed by the infinitive without *to*. We use didn't with *I, you, he/she/it, we* and *they*.

Anna doesn't (does not) live with her dad.

Derek didn't (did not) go to the climbing wall with Anna.

We add not after the main verbs *be, can,* and *could*. We usually use the contracted form –n't.

Penny wasn't (was not) born in Sarajevo.

Selim couldn't (could not) find a job easily.

3 Write the negative form of the sentences.

a Anna could tell her dad about Selim.

  ..... *Anna couldn't tell her dad about Selim.* .....

b Anna was going to make dinner with Penny.

  ....

c Derek works for a Bosnian company.

  ....

d Last year the sales figures were very good.

  ....

e Jill went climbing at the weekends.

  ....

f One weekend after climbing, Jill was at home.

  ....

g Anna wanted to read the letter from Jill.

  ....

h Anna knew about Jill and Lars.

  ....

i Jill came back to live with Derek and Anna.

  ....

j Anna could make Derek think differently.

  ....

GRAMMAR CHECK

Position of adjectives

We use adjectives to describe people and things. Adjectives come after the verb *be* and/or before a noun. When we use two, or more, adjectives with the verb *be*, we link them with *and*.

Selim was good-looking and kind.

When we use two, or more, adjectives before a noun we link them with a comma.

Selim was a kind, good-looking man.

4 **Correct the mistakes in the sentences. There may be more than one mistake in some of the sentences.**

a One day Selim had a letter and he ~~was~~ angry.

b 'He's an immigrant illegal,' they said.

c Some British people don't like foreigners because they different are.

d Selim was sad, angry.

e When he drove to Wales, Dad excited and happy.

f The rocks on Tryfan wet dangerous were.

g When they were on Tryfan, Anna worried was because her dad tired.

h Selim has got hair dark and eyes blue.

i Selim a good climber.

j Anna doesn't want to tell her dad about Selim because his name not English.

5 **Make adjectives from the red words. Then rewrite the sentences using an adjective.**

a Tryfan is a mountain in **Wales**. ......*Tryfan is a Welsh mountain.*......

b Selim is an immigrant from **Bosnia**. ....

c Derek works for a company from **Sweden**. ....

d Anna climbs **well**. ....

e Selim has got good **looks**. ....

GRAMMAR CHECK

Past Simple: affirmative and negative

To make the Past Simple affirmative we add –d or –ed to regular verbs.

Anna worked hard for her exams.   Selim phoned Anna in the evening.

Some regular verbs like *hug, plan,* and *slip* double the final consonant before we add –ed. Irregular verbs have different endings. You must learn the Past Simple forms.

be – I was very tired.   go – I went home for Christmas.

To make the Past Simple negative we use didn't + infinitive without *to*.

He didn't listen.

The Past Simple negative of *be* is wasn't/weren't.

Dad wasn't there.   My exams weren't easy.

6 Write the Past Simple form of the verbs.

   a forget *forgot*   **f** leave ....

   b slip ....   **g** miss ....

   c give ....   **h** hug ....

   d climb ....   **i** hate ....

   e buy ....   **j** plan ....

7 Complete the sentences with the verbs in the box below. Use the affirmative or negative form of the Past Simple. Use some of the verbs twice.

argue	*be*	find	give	go	leave	meet	speak	tell

   a Anna's exams *weren't* easy.

   b Anna .... Selim a phone number for an organization.

   c Anna .... home for Christmas.

   d Dad .... Anna at the bus station.

   e Things .... easy for Derek at the factory.

   f Anna and Derek .... on Christmas Day.

   g Anna .... Derek about her boyfriend.

   h Two days later, Anna .... home and .... back to Oxford.

   i Anna .... a room in a house to rent.

   j Derek .... to Anna when she phoned home.

GRAMMAR CHECK

Linkers: before, after, and when

We can link two sentences about actions in the past using before, after, or when. We use when to link two actions that happened close in time.

Anna and Derek argued. She didn't hear from him for a long time.

After Anna and Derek argued, she didn't hear from him for a long time.

Dad hugged Selim. His face went red.

Dad's face went red when he hugged Selim.

Before Anna met Selim, she didn't know much about Bosnia.

With the linking word at the start of the sentence, we put a comma after the first clause.

8 Link the two sentences using the word in brackets.

a We said goodbye to Jane. She went shopping. (after)

..After we said goodbye to Jane, she went shopping...

b Anna and Selim put helmets on. They began climbing Tryfan. (before)

c Anna looked up. A rock fell down from the top of the mountain. (when)

d Anna stopped falling down. She heard Selim's voice. (after)

e Anna swung at the rock wall three times. She caught the big rock. (after)

f They didn't know if Derek was dead or alive. Selim climbed down to him. (before)

g Anna found Dad's phone. She phoned the Mountain Rescue people. (when)

h The helicopter left. Selim spoke to Anna. (after)

i Selim's father gave his mother a ring. They were married. (before)

j Anna opened the small green box. There was a beautiful ring in it. (when)

GRAMMAR

GRAMMAR CHECK

Linkers: but, because, and so

We use linkers to join two sentences.

but links two sentences with different ideas.

There were lots of people at the bar, <u>but Anna pushed to the front</u>.
(second sentence shows a different idea)

We use so to add a sentence that explains a result.

Anna didn't like drunk men <u>so she pushed past him</u>.
(result of first part of sentence)

We use because to add a sentence that explains a reason.

Sebastian was angry <u>because Anna's Coke went over his shirt</u>.
(reason for first part of sentence)

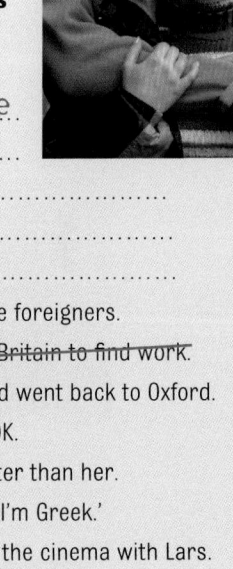

9 **Match sentence halves a–j with 1–10. Write complete sentences using *but*, *so*, or *because*.**

a Selim couldn't find a job in Sarajevo

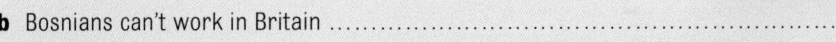
Selim couldn't find a job in Sarajevo so he came to Britain to find work.

b Bosnians can't work in Britain ....

c Anna is a good climber ....

d Anna couldn't tell Derek about Selim ....

e Anna's mum wasn't interested in climbing

....

f Selim was angry ....

....

g Anna and Derek stopped climbing Tryfan

....

h Derek was happier than usual ....

....

i Derek and Anna argued on Christmas Day

....

j A rock fell and hit Derek on the head ....

....

1 He didn't like foreigners.

2 ~~He came to Britain to find work.~~

3 Anna left and went back to Oxford.

4 Derek was OK.

5 Selim is better than her.

6 Selim says, 'I'm Greek.'

7 She went to the cinema with Lars.

8 Anna went to Wales and didn't stay with him.

9 Anna couldn't tell him about Selim.

10 It was wet and dangerous.

DOMINOES
THE STRUCTURED APPROACH TO READING IN ENGLISH

Dominoes is an enjoyable series of illustrated classic and modern stories in four carefully graded language stages – from Starter to Three – which take learners from beginner to intermediate level.

Each *Domino* reader includes:
- **a good story** to read and enjoy
- **integrated activities** to develop reading skills and increase active vocabulary
- **personalized projects** to make the language and story themes more meaningful
- **seven pages of grammar activities** for consolidation.

Each *Domino* pack contains a reader, plus a MultiROM with:
- **a complete audio recording of the story**, fully dramatized to bring it to life
- **interactive activities** to offer further practice in reading and language skills and to consolidate learning.

If you liked this Level One *Domino*, why not read these?

Deep Trouble
Lesley Thompson

Amy and Matt are bored. They don't want to study for their exams. They want to have a good time. So they drive to the marina at West Palm Beach, and Matt jumps onto one of the boats. 'We can go anywhere!' he jokes.

But when the owners of the boat come back and find them, Amy and Matt are in deep trouble. Matt is a good swimmer and enjoys scuba-diving, but now he must dive for their lives.

Book ISBN: 978 0 19 424761 0
MultiROM Pack ISBN: 978 0 19 424725 2

The Real McCoy & Other Ghost Stories
Lesley Thompson

'Are you scared, Gordon?' asks Heather.

Four friends talk of ghosts in a hotel in Scotland. That night Gordon sees and hears something strange in his room. But is it really the ghost of Lord McCoy?

These six stories tell of ghosts – friendly, sad, and bad – from Britain, Australia, New Zealand, America – and Egypt!

Book ISBN: 978 0 19 424767 2
MultiROM Pack ISBN: 978 0 19 424731 3

You can find details and a full list of books in the *Dominoes* catalogue and Oxford English Language Teaching Catalogue, and on the website: www.oup.com/elt

Teachers: see www.oup.com/elt for a full range of online support, or consult your local office.

	CEF	Cambridge Exams	IELTS	TOEFL iBT	TOEIC
Starter	A1	YLE Movers	–	–	–
Level 1	A1–A2	YLE Flyers/KET	3.0	–	–
Level 2	A2–B1	KET-PET	3.0-4.0	–	–
Level 3	B1	PET	4.0	57-86	550